Mana Magic

The Huna philosophy is a comprehensive and enlightening model for self-understanding. John Bainbridge has summarized its usefulness in a remarkably succinct way, and has integrated Vector, a modern method for removing unconscious barriers. The result is a specific technique for manifesting one's experience in the way he or she would like. From the treatment of disease to the improvement of one's daily circumstances, these practical tools are ready and waiting.

> *Ronald L. Peters, M.D.*
> *Medical Director, Innerhealth*
> *Center, Los Angeles, CA.*

"This book presents a condensed, yet lucid explanation of ancient metaphysical principles. Further, it introduces Vector, a contemporary method of personal problem solving which is as effective as it is simple."

> *Brian J. Perry, Ph.D., J.D.*

Mana Magic

How You Can Use The Powerful Huna Secret of Ancient Hawaii in Today's High-Tech World

by John Bainbridge

Barnhart Press, Los Angeles, CA

For information address Barnhart Press, P.O. Box 27940
Los Angeles, CA 90027

See Appendix for ordering information

Design by Bonita Montano, Aloha Designs, Glendale, CA.

Library of Congress Cataloging in Publication Data

Bainbridge, John
  Mana Magic
Includes Index

1. Hawaiian Magic   2. Huna Magic   3. Kahuna Magic
I. Title

ISBN 0-9620658-0-3

Library of Congress Catalog Card Number: 88-70689

Manufactured in the United States of America
Barnhart Press, P.O. Box 27940, Los Angeles, CA 90027
First Barnhart Press Edition: June 1988

10 9 8 7 6 5 4 3 2 1

The graphic symbol of three interlocking circles and a dot in the center is a registered service mark of of the Vector Church. Application has been made to the United States Patent Office (June, 1988) for registration of the name Vector as a service name for The Presiding Vector of the Vector Church (incorporated in California in 1967).

DEDICATION

This book is dedicated to all those people, kahuna and others, who have preserved the coded secret of Mana Magic through the ages, and to Max Freedom Long, who deciphered it, reconstructed it as "Huna" and presented it to the world.

FOREWORD

"Mana Magic" is indeed a clear, simple explanation of how you can use the powerful Huna secret of Ancient Hawaii in today's high-tech world, just as the subtitle suggests. It consists of easy-to-follow instructions, and it has a unique feature which perhaps only this author could have included. That is the "cleansing" (*kala* in Hawaiian) technique known as Vector.

John Bainbridge is qualified both as a Huna teacher and as a Vector counselor. Often Huna students use our techniques quite easily until they encounter a blocked path to the high self. Of the various methods of *kala*, Vector is one of the simplest and most effective ways of accomplishing that important step toward goal attainment.

This is a valuable book which you will want to keep with you. As with most worthwhile endeavors, you still have to work at Huna, but it can improve your life so much that you will be thankful this Mana Magic secret has survived through the ages.

> Dr. E. Otha Wingo,
> Executive Director
> HUNA RESEARCH, INC.

TABLE OF CONTENTS

Chapter	Contents	Page
1	Introduction (Orientation to the Secret) ...	1
2	Aloha (Many Benefits for You)	9
3	What is Mana?	11
4	What is Magic?	13
5	Origins of the Secret	15
6	The Secret's Survival Through the Ages ...	19
7	The Secret Forbidden	21
8	The Secret Reconstructed	23
9	The Secret Revealed	25
10	Understanding the Secret	27
11	How to Use the Secret	31
	• Teamwork Required	31
	• Preview of the Ha Rite	32
	• Composing Your Request	33
12	The Problem of the Complex	37
	• The Basic Self's Rigid Concepts	37
	• Traditional Methods of Changing Concepts	38
	• Searching for a More Efficient Method	39
13	New! Using Vector to Dissolve Complexes	41
	• Vector Emerges	41
	• Identifying a Complex's Pattern	42
	• Finding the Complex's Beginning	45
	• Isolating the Complex's Components	48
	• Disposing of Those Components	49
	• Questions? Answers:	50

TABLE OF CONTENTS
(Continued)

14 Conducting the Ha Rite 57
• Choosing Your Setting 57
• Generating Mana 58
• Offering Up Mana 59
• Adding Pictures 59
• Giving Thanks 60
15 Persisting/Insisting 65
• Results? How Soon? 65
• Any "Eating Companions" Around? 66
• Adjust Your Karma? 66
16 Success Stories 67
17 Aloha Nui Loa 75
Appendix 77
Glossary 80
Index 83

LIST OF ILLUSTRATIONS

Mountains 1
Mountains (Expanded View) 8
Hawaiian Petroglyph 9
Triform Waves (Mana) 11
Triform Waves (Mana) 12
Tapa (Symbol) 13
Hawaiian Orchid 14
Hieroglyphics 15
Tapa (Symbol) 17
Tapa (Leaf) 18
Hawaiian Petroglyph (Symbol) 19
Hawaiian Petroglyph 20
Church 21
Hawaiian Foliage 22
Max Freedom Long 23
Moon Over Bamboo 24
Energy Focus Symbol 25
Tapa (Symbol) 26
Ten-and-Three Symbol 27
Chart: Ten Components 30
Rowers (Teamwork) 31
King Kamehameha 36
Hawaiian Petroglyph 37
Museum Tapa 40
Vector Symbol 41
Chart: Elements of a Complex 44
Outline: Vector Counseling Method 53
Vector Logo (Expanded) 54
Mask by Author 56
Hawaiian Petroglyph 59
Hawaiian Petroglyph 60

LIST OF ILLUSTRATIONS
(Continued)

Diagram: Failed Ha Rite 61
Diagram: Successful Ha Rite 62
Flow Chart of the Ha Rite 63
Sphinx 65
Sphinx (Profile) 66
Happy Sun 67
Hawaiian Petroglyph 73
Computer Circuitry 74
Alii Figure 75
Polynesian Boating Party 76

Chapter 1

Introduction

 Mana Magic can be of the greatest benefit to you. Let me tell you how I found out about it, what it did for me and why I want to pass the secret on to you.

The fact that you are interested in this subject probably means that you have a problem or two which you have not solved by conventional means. Problems come in all sizes, of course, but to each person his or her allotment seems large enough.

That's how my share seemed to me as I struggled through the years to solve problems of health, income and personal relationships. After I began to make a little progress in my own uphill battle, I asked myself the age-old question, "Is there a greater meaning to life—something more significant and enjoyable—than merely staying alive to earn a living, getting married, raising a family, being saddled with debts, having some enjoyable experiences, suffering bitter disappointments, then getting old and dying?"

Many people seem resigned to that, or to a similar scenario. A great many other people apparently give the matter little, if any, thought.

A large percentage of the world's population, how-ever, turns to religion to tell them about the meaning of life and how to regard their problems. Some such seekers who ask penetrating questions do not find satisfactory answers there. Instead, they often dis-cover disappointing religious histories of originally simple, problem-solving teachings which have been distorted and fragmented through the centuries. Frozen into rigid belief systems, such dogmas keep their adherents in ignorance and subject them to artificially-created feelings of guilt, fear and inadequacy.

That is not to say that religions have given no comfort or performed no helpful works. Neither is this to impugn the high ideals advocated by most of them. If you are involved with a religion or a philo-sophy which provides all the answers you require, and gives you the means with which to solve your problems, then by all means stay with it.

The dogmas of most religions preclude their hav-ing any interest in looking at the premises of Mana Magic. Neither is physical science motivated to investigate areas of the paranormal, because its phenomena are not clearly measurable. They are not explainable by current scientific theory, nor are they reliably reproducible by any and all experimenters under laboratory conditions.

I have great respect for science. However, it seems true that there is a lot more to "reality" than our five senses can detect directly, or even by using state-of-the-art electronic instrumentation.

Thus, it is without regard for the purely intellectual constraints set by physical science, or the doctrinal censorship imposed by religions that this journey of discovery begins.

As you prepare to take your first upward steps on this trail, give careful consideration to where you want to go, figuratively speaking, and where you are at present along "The Way".

An allegory from the Island of Molokai may help you do that, just as it has served the purpose of explaining to Hawaiian school children the differences between Hawaiian and haole (foreigners') perceptions of the history of the Islands.

Told to me by a wise Hawaiian friend, it goes (somewhat modified) like this:

> "When you begin to climb a mountain you have no vistas, only a sense of where you are going. After you have traveled awhile you can see from whence you came, and you have some perspective of where you are going. You may glimpse other travelers below you, or above you, who are climbing the same mountain.

> "When you are half way to the top, you can see far down the mountain side and off into the distance. Other wayfarers however, have taken different pathways, and to each the view is different, although you are all climb-

ing the same mountain. Some journeyers may get lost. A few may stop climbing. Some may choose much more rewarding pathways than the others do.

"When you reach the peak, you see the magnificent, overall panorama. You can also see and understand each view of each traveler—all correct from the point at which each stood at any given moment during the journey."

That figurative mountain, which we are all climbing, represents "The Way". At a certain point in my own journey toward that imaginary peak, having already explored many byways, I paused once again, studied the now greatly expanded view, and found that my attention was clearly focused on reports of certain esoteric, magical practices of the ancient Hawaiians. As I delved into the subject, my fascination with it grew, because of its logical simplicity and great problem-solving potential.

Somewhere on that trail, long, long ago, even though they possessed no electronic measuring devices or sophisticated mathematical skills, certain of the ancients discovered a creative life force which the Polynesians called *"mana"* (mah'-nah). They learned how to work with it to help them solve the problems of their day. Millenia later, this well-kept secret came to the attention of an American investigator.

That inquiring scholar was Max Freedom Long, who spent many years reconstructing the rapidly disappearing remnants of the ancient magic. He felt that information of such value should not be lost to the world. The ages-old mystery had no name, so he called his rediscovery *"Huna"* (who'-nah), an Hawaiian word, one meaning of which is "secret".

It is my purpose in this work to synthesize thousands of hours of research and present to you an updated, concise report of the essence of the series of books which Max Freedom Long wrote several decades ago.

Here you will find a background summary and a brief, understandable explanation of Huna theory, together with instructions and illustrative diagrams. This combination is designed to enable you to begin making practical use of the system.

Thus, in this age of revelations, Huna—"the secret"—has now become "that which is to be revealed."

Such revelations come to each of us when we are ready to recognize them. I was not ready in 1947 when my mother—who was always fascinated by new discoveries—excitedly informed me that she had just met a researcher/writer named Max Freedom Long who had recently written a book about his re-discovery of the secret, "workable" magic system of the ancient Hawaiians. She had a copy and asked if I wanted to read it.

"No, thanks," I said. I was much too busy starting a career in advertising and being a new father. I could spare no time for something which I thought would be of no practical value.

Twenty years went by, and things were going badly for me. I had lost my job and our home. My wife and I were divorced and my debts had become a monstrous burden. 1967 was indeed a low point in my life. Then, one day in a public library, my attention was drawn to a copy of Max Freedom Long's "Secret Science Behind Miracles," and I remembered that it was the book my mother had told me about years before. I read and re-read it. I began practicing what it taught. My situation quickly began to improve.

Using the Mana Magic of Huna became a way of life for me. As though by magic, I easily found appropriate and remunerative employment. I began to pay off all my debts, karmic and otherwise. My personal and social life evolved from chaos into order. I put my years of study to work and became a certified Huna teacher and practitioner. I started a consulting business which grew each year.

As another two decades passed, the ancient Huna Magic continued to improve my life, but there were still obstructions. I realized that I had not resolved certain inner complexities, and that such omission was keeping me from attaining the peace and power I needed to truly prosper. I felt that to cope effectively with the pressurized events in today's fast-moving, stressful, high-tech world, I needed a practical, contemporary, complex-clearing technique.

I searched for such a treasure, and I found it.

This unique, twentieth century system for ridding yourself of unrewarding, unwanted and self-defeating attitudes and behavior patterns (complexes) is called "Vector". This Mana Magic booklet contains the information you need in order to use Vector as a powerful component of this updated Huna procedure.

By means of this dual approach—ancient Huna plus modern Vector, which is offered authentically here (and nowhere else)—you can soon learn how easily and legitimately you can lay down the cumbersome and unnecessary psychic burdens which may be troubling you and cluttering up your life.

If you have a trusted, like-minded friend, it can be helpful for you to work together on this program. Otherwise, as for discussing any important secret you may have with strangers or anyone who may scoff at it, the probable result would be to lessen its usefulness to you.

Having explored and followed this pathway for a number of years, my seemingly unsolvable problems are now happily resolved. My business and my personal life are flourishing. By knowing and using this combination of ancient and modern secrets and techniques, I assure you that you too can make rapid and enjoyable progress along "The Way".

Are you ready to start your journey? If so, "E hoomaka!" (eh-ho-oh-mah'-kah). That's Hawaiian for "Begin!"

Chapter 2

Aloha

Aloha. Greetings! I bring you good news! You have a miraculously powerful ally who can solve your problems and change the way things happen to you (and for you!). Do you have a genuine desire to heal some physical, mental or psychic condition? To improve or change some relationship? To reduce stress? To increase confidence? To better your financial condition or your love life? To resolve a difficult karma? To achieve a greater understanding of your being? To accomplish real spiritual growth?

That powerful ally can bring about these and other desired changes in your life . . . under certain conditions. You must know how to:

(1) make your request
(2) generate the necessary power ("mana")
(3) clear your pathway of complexes (mental obstructions)
(4) avoid hurting anyone in the process

That powerful ally is your own high self or superconscious; In Hawaiian: *aumakua:* (ah'-oo-mahkoo'-

ah). However, it is not your babysitter. Its function is to foster your evolution by letting you learn life's lessons at your own pace. It must, therefore, use its awesome, creative power to construct your day-to-day future in accordance with the messages which you are constantly sending it.

This Mana Magic discourse explains that relationship. Of the world's thousands of philosophies, religions, psychological schools of thought, cults, shamanic magic systems and contemporary self-help programs, the equal opportunity principles of Mana Magic—neither racist nor sexist—appear to be the most ancient, the least difficult and the most effective. They are now available to any individual seeker.

Following this path is a liberating and enlightening experience. Neither religious, in a dogmatic sense, nor anti-religious, in any sense, Mana Magic enables you to take the responsibility for proceeding confidently toward a mature, goal-oriented independence of your own choosing.

On the other hand, if you would not yet feel comfortable being totally independent, this Mana Magic practice can serve to protect you from being victimized by unscrupulous cults or leaders. It can help you to gravitate toward appropriate individuals and/or groups which will be caring and genuinely helpful, whatever your present stage of spiritual development may be.

Chapter 3

What is Mana?

The Polynesian word "mana" is listed similarly in several dictionaries. Thus, a definition would be "a generalized, supernatural force which may be concentrated in certain objects and in people, endowing those who possess it with extraordinary powers." Where did that idea come from and how does one get to "possess" mana?

Allegorical references to Breath and Light were sacred components of the ancient Hawaiian creation chants. Note this interesting parallel: According to the Gospel of St. John (I, 1), "In the beginning was the word . . ."

Similarly, according to Hawaiian family historian and author, Kauakokoula Kuhaimoana Kaimana Willis of the Paia-Kapela-Willis 'Ohana (known to his friends as "Koko"), their ancestral chant said, "In the beginning was the *'ha'*"—meaning the divine breath of life. (Inference: In order for there to be "The Word," must there also not be "the breath?").

That chant goes on to relate that ". . . the Light

observed the land and it was good. A shadow fell across the flat land *(alo)*. The Light bent over to look at it and breathed upon the Earth and the Earth sprang to life."

Thus, out of sacred tradition was the word *"alo-ha"* born, and from it the concept of deep breathing to generate/concentrate mana, that pervasive power that can bring about desired transformations.

Actually, the idea of a universal, primordial force is not limited to Polynesia. It is a world-wide concept.

Is there more than one type of etheric energy, or is "mana" the ancient name for the same cosmic force which Yoga conceives of as "prana," which the martial arts call "chi" or "ki," which the Iroquois Indians called "orenda," which nineteenth century German physicist Baron Karl von Reichenbach labeled as "odic force," which twentieth century psychoanalyst Dr. Wilhelm Reich perceived as "orgone energy," and to which other discoverers around the world have given other names?

Until there exists a scientifically recognized way to measure those energies, who can say? Meanwhile, knowledgeable practitioners continue to use it, whatever its scientific definition may eventually turn out to be.

Chapter 4

What is Magic?

 There is an abundance of literature on all aspects of the universally intriguing subject of magic. Max Freedom Long (MFL) certainly found it fascinating. Early in his research of how the *kahuna* had practiced their brand of magic, he learned that those Polynesian adepts had to use some kind of force or "invisible substance" to accomplish their results.

That enabling force was mana. MFL speculated that it was probably akin to electricity or magnetism, and like those other, more apparent natural energies, mana was neither "good" nor "bad." It was neutral.

This Mana Magic presentation reports on the powerful, benign aspects of the use of mana, and employs the term "magic" in its broad and ancient sense of a seemingly inexplicable power which can change things.

That concept is embodied in the expressions "the magic of love," "the magic of prayer," and "the magic of faith."

Chapter 5

Origins of the Secret

 Where did the secret of Mana Magic originate? According to the writings of MFL, the American scholar who devoted his life to "Recovering the Ancient Magic" (the title of his first book), it existed at least as far back as ancient Egypt, and probably long before that.

There has been romantic speculation concerning the origin of the secret. Did it begin on the postulated, long-submerged continent of Lemuria (Mu)? Was it a product of the legendary, antedeluvian continent of Atlantis? Was it imported to Earth by extraterrestrial immigrants? All of the above? None of the above?

However remote (or near) its ultimate genesis might have been, let's get on with this report and pick up the trail at some point in dynastic Egypt, as MFL did, and inquire how the secret was kept alive, and whether it is of any practical value today.

MFL's observations regarding the symbology of the pictographs decorating the walls of certain

Egyptian tombs convinced him that the secret was known to some individuals and was transmitted to knowledgeable members of future generations by means of a secret, unchanging, coded *language-within-a-language*.

Years later, discouraged by his apparent lack of progress, after he had almost given up his quest, he was led, he felt, to undertake an exhaustive philological dissection of the agglutinative Hawaiian language. That is, he interpreted the definitions of short words which retained their meanings, even when they were combined as syllables to make up longer words having different meanings.

MFL further theorized that various groups of ancient Egyptian "keepers of the secret" emigrated, over a long period of time, in several directions.

For our purpose, let's track those people who generation by generation, appear gradually to have made their way, via India, and then Indonesia, to New Zealand, Tahiti. and certain other islands in the Pacific Ocean. By incredibly skillful feats of navigation, some of those hardy ancestors of the Polynesians, in open canoes, without compasses, traveled northward across the Pacific Ocean until they reached the lush and uninhabited Hawaiian Islands. Those who settled there, and their descendants, became known as *Maoli* (mah-oh'-lee)—the ancient ones. They also called themselves the Mu.

In that tropical paradise, for an undetermined period of time, the *Maoli* lived happy, peaceful lives, in balanced harmony with nature's animal, vegetable and mineral kingdoms. There, they practiced and preserved the ancient secret, by oral tradition (exact, word-for-word memorization of the coded language—they had no written language) in their extended-family society.

Eventually, trouble literally appeared on the horizon in the form of an invading army of fierce warriors arriving in a flotilla of huge war canoes.

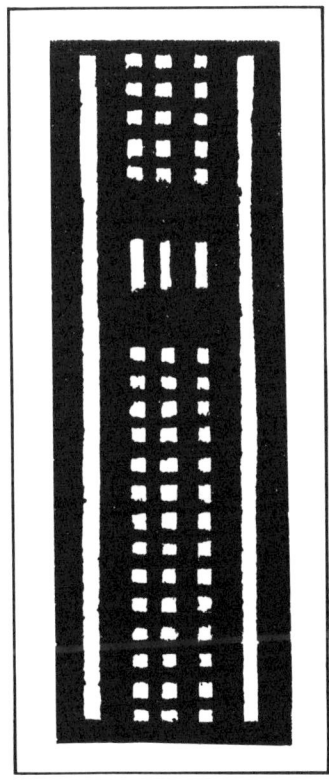

Chapter 6

The Secret's Survival Through the Ages

 Knowledge of early Hawaiian history is sketchy at best, but according to the family records of Koko, referred to in the previous chapter, it was about the middle of the twelfth century, A.D., that a large force of Polynesian invaders from Tahiti conquered Hawaii.

They superimposed on the benign social structure of the *Maoli,* their own harsh *Alii* (ah-lee'-ee) caste system.

Alii means "chief." They declared themselves the chiefs and relegated the *Maoli* to lower class status.

The secret became corrupted on Hawaii, as it had elsewhere in the world. Some *Maoli,* however, managed to keep it alive, in that coded, secret language, in its pure form.

As was frequently the case in historical conqueror/vanquished situations, accommodations took place and life went on. In the Hawaiian social structure, there continued to be several classes of experts, including those priestly "keepers of the secret" known as *kahuna* (kah-who'-nah—there is no "s" to denote plurals in Hawaiian).

Through life-long training and practice, certain *kahuna* priests became such adept manipulators of mana that they reportedly could use it to communicate telepathically with each other and with various other life forms (ancestral spirits, sharks, porpoises and birds); to walk barefoot, without harm, on fire-hot lava flows (firewalking is now being performed by an increasing number of people, worldwide); to influence the weather; to effect instant healings; to induce pre-cognitive visions and even to bring about desired changes in the perceived future.

Chapter 7

The Secret Forbidden

 In the early 19th century, some influential Hawaiians invited missionaries from the USA to come to the islands and Christianize the population. Thus it was in 1820 that the first group of Congregationalist missionaries arrived from New England.

They were welcomed in the true aloha spirit and immediately set about making converts. Since that was specifically their mission, they had no motivation to try to understand the islanders' perceptions of how humans interact with nature and with higher powers. The Hawaiian pantheon of elemental spirits, gods and goddesses—including the Big Four, Ku, Kane, Lono, and Kanaloa—appeared to the newcomers not as symbols, such as some Christian religious icons and statues, but rather as mere heathen idolotry.

The missionaries were pleased to find that the Hawaiian king had already ended the ancient system of *kapu* (kah'poo), whereby specified foods and activities were forbidden to certain classes of people, and where men and women were forbidden to eat together.

However, the sin-oriented New Englanders found the otherwise happy, easygoing ways of the natives quite shocking, so they quickly imposed their stern, no-nonsense, nineteenth century Protestant values on the hapless, scantily-clad islanders.

The Yale-educated missionaries also addressed themselves to the task of devising an alphabet and writings a dictionary for the spoken Hawaiian language, so that they could translate the Bible for their new converts.

Even while paganism was in the process of giving way to Congregationalism (other religions came later), *kahunaism* continued to thrive as it always had. The missionaries, of course—incorrectly—equated those magical practices with what they considered to be witchcraft and devil worship.

In a determined effort to stamp it out, they persuaded the Hawaiian king to declare *kahunaism* to be a major crime. That proscription convinced many Christian converts to abandon it, but the ancient tradition did not entirely die out. No longer practiced openly, *kahunaism* languished underground.

Chapter 8

The Secret Reconstructed

In 1917, a young American school teacher, MFL, accepted a teaching job in Hawaii. There, he became fascinated with the islands' history and culture, especially with the veiled references he heard pertaining to the (still illegal) practices of the *kahuna*. From that time to his death in 1970, MFL devoted his life to recovering the ancient secret. His intensive study of the Hawaiian language and its age-old chants, plus his years of consultation with elderly Hawaiians, provided him with the basis for restructuring "the secret," which had no name until he called it "Huna."

MFL was also an avid student of comparative religions, theosophy, hypnosis, and the abundance of early twentieth century literature pertaining to the paranormal: channeling, crystals, pendulums, etc.

With that broad background, MFL authored a series of books on *Huna* (see Appendix). Specifically disavowing any intention of starting a cult, he also formed an international association of interested people around the world—Huna Research Associates—who experimented with Huna and, according to their correspondence, found it to be a very "workable" system. That is, they reported having achieved success with certain psi activities such as telepathy, clairvoyance, map dowsing, healing, etc.

Furthermore, MFL clearly recognized that he was a pioneer in this area of rediscovery. He anticipated that as others take up the work where he left off, and as scientific evidence begins to confirm his thesis, the result could well be a Renaissance of Huna.

Chapter 9

The Secret Revealed

 Ever since the U.S. Congress removed the criminalizing, nineteenth century stigma on Huna and similar practices by passing the Native American Religions Act in the 1970's, many versions of the ancient Hawaiian practice have emerged.

Some current practitioners refer patronizingly—even distainfully—to MFL's extensive research and writings. Some appear to resent the fact that he presented this secret material so openly to the world. Other writers and lecturers seem to have borrowed freely from MFL's work, some crediting him, others not.

Some twentieth century authorities (including learned Hawaiians) feel that MFL's Huna is really a synthesis of several ancient psychological and metaphysical concepts. Portions of "the secret" can be found in the world's major religions. Some of its principles are readily apparent in the works of contemporary authors of various positive thinking and how-to-succeed courses and publications.

This Mana Magic instruction appreciatively recognizes the fact that MFL was the first researcher/writer to compile this information and publish it in terms comprehensible to the Western mind. This presentation is a careful condensation of the essential elements of MFL's series of books dealing with his reconstruction of ancient Huna. This is the version recognized by Huna Research, Inc., which is the international organization successor to MFL's Huna Research Associates.

Additionally, and exclusively, this instruction offers a uniquely effective new way to clear your blocked path. It shows you how to remove self-defeating attitudes and behavior patterns which may be in your way. That is an essential procedure, as I learned, which must be accomplished before any "magical" or self-help system can be truly effective and lasting.

An appropriate starting point for our explanation is the premise that while the ancients apparently did not speculate on the nature of Ultimate God, they did believe in personal immortality, a spirit world and reincarnation. Furthermore, they conceived of each individual human as being a trinity.

Chapter 10

Understanding the Secret

 This is the Huna concept: a person's body is occupied by, and controlled by, two "selves":

(1) One's "low" self (not meaning unworthy); that is, the unconscious or subconscious; in Hawaiian, "unihipili" (oo-nee-hee-pee'-lee). This "part" of the person, also known as the basic self, exerts a powerful influence on one's life. It is the person's animal nature, and is in charge of the body's autonomic nervous system, memory banks, dreams, emotions, telepathic and other psi (psychic) abilities.

(2) One's "middle" self or conscious self—"uhane" (oo-hah'-nay)—that is, the thinking, rational part of the individual. It is responsible for making the logical decisions in the person's life. Another aspect of the conscious self's "job" is to control and educate the basic self. In a normal, well person, the conscious and unconscious components work harmoniously together.

A third member of the trinity, one's high self,

conceptually, hovers above the body, which houses the middle self and the basic self. The high self is the person's super-conscious—aumakua (ah-oo-mah-koo'-ah)—and may be thought of as one's guardian angel.

The high self is connected to the middle self, not directly, but via the basic self, by an infinitely extendable shadowy cord—the aka (ah'-kah) cord. In western societies, it became known as the "silver cord." MFL describes the super-conscious as androgynous (male and female, united), an enormously powerful, "utterly trustworthy parental pair."

Each of the person's three-in-one entities is described, from an earthly viewpoint, as being interpenetrated or surrounded by a "subtle" or "shadow" body—an aka-body—which is an etheric duplicate. Another way of stating this relationship is that one's earthly body is a physical manifestation of one's etheric body.

Is it a representation of the shadow body of the middle self or the basic self, or of both, which Kirlian (see Glossary) photographs capture, and which some people can see as an aura?

Also, each of the person's three-in-one entities works with its own kind of power. Mana is the basic force. It is thought of as being universally pervasive. As such, it is routinely absorbed or collected and concentrated by the basic self, as needed, to sustain life.

The conscious self converts mana to *mana-mana*

or brain power. Brain-waves, of course, can be recorded on an encephalograph.

The high self makes use of the basic mana by amplifying it many, many times, transforming it into mana-loa (mah'-nah low'-ah), the "highest" force. These three degrees of power might be likened to electrical voltages: 110, 220 and the ultimately high voltages carried by high tension wires.

Thus, there are ten different but interacting elements which constitute the Huna system: a super conscious or high self; a conscious, or middle self; and a basic, or "low" self. Each "self" has its own duplicate shadow body and each works with its own degree of power, or *mana*. These, plus the physical body, add up to ten integrated components. This concept is basic to Huna.

The ancients were also aware of various other types of non-physical entities; some, low-level discarnate beings (having no physical body); others, even more highly advanced than the high selves— those constituting an ever-upward-evolving, heavenly hierarchy. When necessary, your high self can intercede on your behalf as far up the line as may be appropriate.

Another concept was "the great company of high selves—*poe aumakua* (poh'-ay ah-oo-mah-koo'-ah) —that is, any group of high selves networking together on some project for their earthly charges. (See Diagram of Huna Concept of a Human Entity).

DIAGRAM OF A PERSON'S
10 COMPONENTS

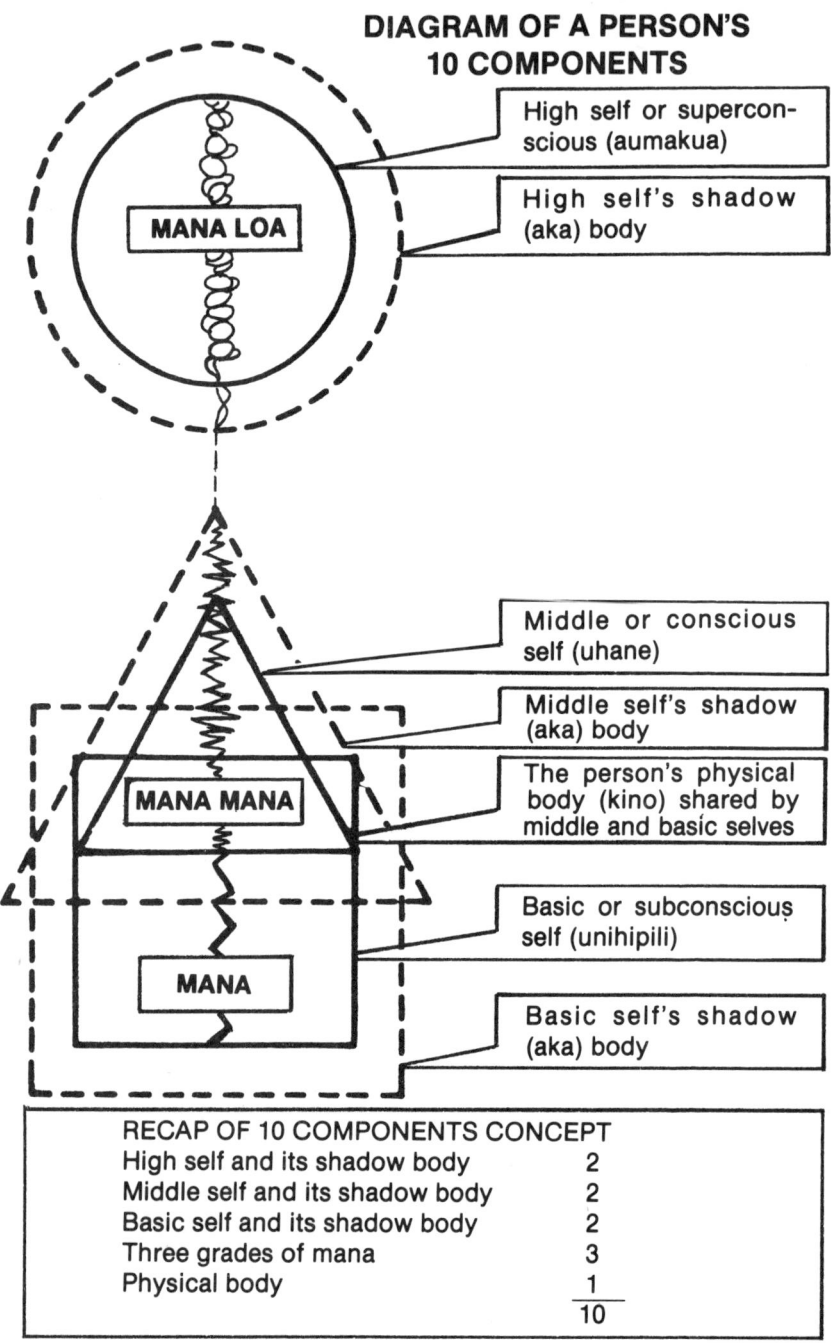

High self or supercon-
scious (aumakua)

High self's shadow
(aka) body

Middle or conscious
self (uhane)

Middle self's shadow
(aka) body

The person's physical
body (kino) shared by
middle and basic selves

Basic or subconscious
self (unihipili)

Basic self's shadow
(aka) body

RECAP OF 10 COMPONENTS CONCEPT
High self and its shadow body	2
Middle self and its shadow body	2
Basic self and its shadow body	2
Three grades of mana	3
Physical body	1
	10

Chapter 11

How to Use the Secret

Teamwork Required

Making effective use of the secret depends on your getting your "three selves" working together in harmony. Your high self can only use its enormous power to bring about the changes you want in your life when it receives your request to do so. Remember, your high self shapes each of your tomorrows as you (conscious self and basic self) visualize them, without regard for how "good" or "bad," how hit-or-miss each tomorrow may seem. You are learning life's lessons at your own pace. However, your high self does intervene in cases where your physical life is in danger, but it is not yet time for your earthly life to end.

If you are sufficiently unhappy with some aspect(s) of your life, you can ask your high self for help any time you are ready. How do you make that request? By means of a prayer, but in a form quite different from the usual concept of a supplicant devoutly verbalizing a petition to Ultimate God (or to some other member of the heavenly hierarchy). That type of prayer often includes a statement of the petitioner's problem together with a reaffirmation of his or her being a miserable sinner.

As a result of that emotional exercise, the petitioner's basic self holds on to the problem and intensifies its burden of guilt, fear and unworthiness. Such a prayer, no matter how sincerely uttered, will probably not be effective because it doesn't "go" anywhere.

What does the *Huna* prayer—also called a ha-rite—do differently? "Ha" means "strong breathing." That, plus a type of affirmation and vivid visualization, are essential, but the process consists of more than that, as you will see in the following pages.

As you state the Huna prayer, you picture your desired result, in positive form, as an accomplished fact. You send that mental image "up" the connecting *aka* cord on a great surcharge of mana, to your high self. If your aka cord is clear of complexes, your high self will receive your prayer and will use the mana on which it traveled to translate your picturization into reality for you. Furthermore, if your high self must send your prayer on up to a still higher authority, it will do so.

Preview of the Ha Rite

Please acquaint yourself with the following overview of the prayer process:

- Prepare a specific prayer request.
- See that your *aka* cord is clear of complexes.

- Specifically generate a greater than normal charge of mana.
- Instruct your basic self to send that surcharge of mana up the *aka* cord to your high self. Visualize that happening.
- Superimpose your visualized prayer (as still or moving pictures) on the surge of mana which you are sending up your *aka* cord. Visualize that happening.
- If your basic self does not perceive your *aka* cord as blocked by complexes, your high self will then make use of the necessary *mana loa* to create for you, in some unknown way—it will probably appear as a coincidence in your life—the new reality you have visualized. Are you ready to proceed?

Compose Your Request

When you (conscious self) are ready to deliver a sincere and heartfelt petition to your high self, you should carefully compose that prayer request. Write it out. Word it precisely. Consider the consequences if it were literally to come true. Is that result really what you want? Be certain that your prayer states clearly and briefly, in positive terms and present tense, exactly what you want to happen.

EXAMPLES:

(1) If you are suffering from some illness, do not say "Heal me of my illness." Rather say, and visualize, something result-oriented, such as "Thank you for keeping me healthy. My (whatever seems to be the

problem) is functioning perfectly," etc. If you feel that you should be seen by a physician or other health professional, by all means, do so. You can still use the prayer to hasten the healing process.

(2) If you need money, do not say, and visualize, "I'm always broke! I need a lot of money!" Rather, state your prayer positively like: "Thank you for the abundance in my life. I earn (a specific number of dollars) per (hour, week, month, year)."

(3) If you are miserable, due to some relationship problem, do not visualize the problem and dwell on it. Don't say "My boss always picks on me," or "I never have any real friends," or "Nobody loves me," etc. Rather, do just the opposite! Say, and see, in your mind's eye, such desired realities as "I behave in such a pleasant way that I get along with practically everybody," or "I can now be a friend to most anybody, and people want to be my friends," or "My personal relationships with (men/women/people) are warm and mutually-rewarding," etc. Elaborate on mental pictures of what you want to manifest and experience in your life.

In composing your prayer, remember that the powerful, high magic process which is being described here is a benign, helpful one. It does not equate with any malevolent magical/psychological systems which invoke the powers of evil and seek revenge or intend harm to others. It is true there are ways of doing that on the low self (unihipili) level—the *ana-ana* (ah-nah' ah-nah') "black magic" death prayer, for example—but no high self would cooperate, and the person engaging in that practice would be inviting appropriate karmic consequences (cosmic retribution— cause and effect). Conversely, if you *kala* (cleanse) yourself properly, as explained below, you cannot be victimized by any other entity, corporeal or incorporeal.

Without requiring any difficult or weird practices, Huna can extend a comprehensive psychic shield of protection for you.

Certainly your prayer requests can pertain to specifically improving any aspect of your life, the lives of your family and friends, the welfare of your community, your nation, the world, etc.

If you are concerned that your prayer for others may interfere somehow with their own karmic need to undergo whatever (unpleasant) experiences they may be having, be reassured. Your high self will send your mana—charged with your visualization for the improvement of the circumstances of other people—to the high selves of those for whom you are praying. There, your prayers will be handled appropriately. Furthermore, those appreciative other high selves will be eager to give any desired assistance to your high self in helping you to achieve your objectives.

After you have written your carefully thought-out prayer, the next step is to "cleanse" yourself; that is, get rid of any complexes which may be obstructing the delivery of your prayer to your high self.

Chapter 12

The Problem of the Complex

The Basic Self's Rigid Concepts

As I became more deeply involved in the study and practice of Huna, I realized that however firm the hold your obstructive complex may have on you, it is indeed necessary to find a way to dissolve it. Even if your complex is the result of your subconscious memories of something traumatic which happened to you during your childhood, you must disassemble it—get rid of it—before your Huna prayer can be truly effective.

In Hawaiian, that procedure is called *"kala"* (kah'-lah), which means to cleanse (yourself). Before you instruct your basic self to present your prayer to your high self, do this: look to see whether you are holding on to any unwanted complexes. Such deep-seated emotions as guilt, fear, grief, anger, apathy and feelings of unworthiness—whether you are harboring them consciously or unconsciously—form an obstructive complex and act as a block, or wall, on your aka cord. That means your basic self will probably be unable to approach your high self to present your carefully prepared prayer visualization.

If you are aware of any problem in your life, take the obvious steps to correct it. If you are treating people hurtfully, stop doing that. Make amends to them if that is possible. If you are taking things that don't belong to you, stop doing that and return what you can. Make restitution. If the people you have hurt are no longer available, at least visualize yourself as mentally apologizing to them. Then, to impress your basic self that you are truly setting things right, give a generous gift to charity.

Also, it helps to go out of your way to do beneficial things for other people, even for strangers. If you are driving a car, be extra polite in traffic. Help a neighbor solve a problem. Assist a handicapped person in some way. Smile at people, and do other kind things. Even so, additional measures are often necessary to complete the cleansing process.

Traditional Methods
of Changing Concepts

In his writings, MFL described a variety of procedures and therapies, both ancient and modern, which individuals and groups have used to try to change behavior patterns—their own and other people's. He reported on hypnotism, Christian Science, Dianetics and the use of affirmations. He told of a traditional, but rather complicated Hawaiian family-group therapy called *hooponopono* (ho-oh-po'-no-po'-no), and of such dramatic and widely used old time Island practices as a kahuna having his client hold his breath while gulping down a mana-charged raw egg, or dunking his head in a calabash of brackish water as long as he could stand it.

Other problem-solving practices have run the gamut—and still do—from a simple belief in the effectiveness of performing certain ritualistic procedures, to the more sophisticated troubled person attending a frequently lengthy and expensive series of professionally conducted therapy sessions.

The menu of techniques is a long one. If any one of them feels correct and works for you, use it.

Searching for a More Efficient Method

My early efforts with Huna, in the 1960's, were hampered by a heavy burden of complexes which were blocking my *aka*-cord. I turned, successively, to several of the above practices, at least the ones which made any sense to me at that time. Some seemed to be partially successful, others not at all. None worked to my satisfaction.

Finally, I was able to state my objective clearly to myself: I was searching for a complex-dissolving technique which would be easy, safe, fast and effective. Then it dawned on me to use the Huna prayer method itself to direct my quest! I did that.

Tapa

Chapter 13

New! Using Vector
To Dissolve Complexes

Vector Emerges

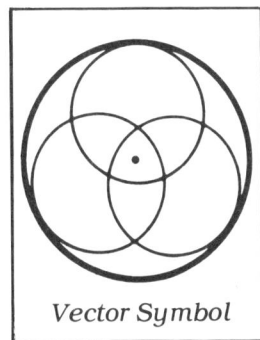

Vector Symbol

Evidently my path (aka cord) wasn't blocked in that regard, for my answer came quickly. Within a few days a friend, knowing nothing of my interest in Huna, happened to introduce me to a brilliant gentleman—he also knew nothing of Huna—who had recently developed exactly the simple, straightforward technique for which I had been searching! His name was George Burtt. A Los Angeles member of Mensa, (the high IQ society), he had spent years studying, analyzing, synthetizing and experimenting with both well known and little known counseling techniques. When he was satisfied with the simplicity and the effectiveness of the method he evolved, he named it "Vector."

Burtt and his friends were already using it with great success. I was most appreciative of his demonstrating to me how I could use his system to disassemble my troubling complexes.

Vector evolved quite independently of Huna, but interestingly, that development took place in the same area of Los Angeles where, years earlier never having heard of Vector, MFL had written his books. Huna, of course, had existed long, long before Vector. Yet, when I looked at those two complementary techniques side by side, they seemed to me like the two sides of the same coin: Side A, a new way to clear the path, and Side B, an ancient way to proceed rapidly and effectively toward one's chosen objectives.

Identifying a Complex's Pattern

My subsequent Vector training and experience taught me that if you want to rid yourself of one or more unwanted complexes, you start by taking a good look at each of them, one at a time. You will soon note that they conform to a common pattern. Each complex is similarly constructed, consisting of four distinct components. Each component can be identified, isolated and disconnected.

During the past quarter-century, Vector practitioners have been quietly perfecting this helpful, non-confrontational counseling technique. They have helped hundreds of people use it to rid themselves of unwanted complexes or behavior patterns. Usually, one correctly conducted session of an hour or so is sufficient to permanently dissolve a complex (get rid of a problem). If you choose to do likewise, here's how:

Look for the pattern of the complex. It consists of four elements:

NK.P!

(1) Your provoking thought or perception which creates the driving emotion(s).
(2) Your emotion(s) which drives your behavior.
(3) Your unwanted behavior and its bodily stress.
(4) The "always" or "never" which holds the pattern together.

Your basic self thinks in those absolute terms.
See following page for typical example.

Three typical examples of the elements of a complex. Remember, your basic self reasons like a computer—in absolute terms.

Possible Provoking Thought	Possible Driving Emotion	Possible Bodily Stress
ALICE: I'll always be sickly. I'll never feel well and strong.	GRIEF	*(Tenaciously holding on to grief)* No matter how hard she tries, Alice's grief drains her energy so that she never has the strength to do the things she wants to do.
BILL: "If I don't succeed in life, I'll end up on skid row!"	FEAR	*(Compulsively striving to acquire)* Bill never has any fun or leisure time because he compulsively devotes all his time and effort to trying to earn more money.
CHARLOTTE: "Every time I get serious about a man, he leaves me!"	ANGER	*(Tensely wanting to, but can't)* Because of her deep-seated anger and accompanying tension, her continual search for the right mate always ends in failure.

Remember, the fourth element of the complex is the "always" or "never."

Finding the Complex's Beginning

After you have identified the pattern, look for its beginning; that is, the first time in your life when you experienced this combination of elements. Any such complex which is giving you serious problems today, almost certainly started in your first few years of life. At that time, your basic self was convinced of some assertion which may, or may not, have been true way back then. In either case, your basic self accepted it as true and generalized it— programmed it into your memory banks for permanent reference. Youyr basic self does, indeed, use that information to affect your life today.

Why? Since you survived that childhood incident, your literal-minded basic self, naive but powerful, believes that your having *that* thought, feeling *that* emotion and engaging in *that* certain behavior is the only way to survive in similar circumstances all through your life. Until, that is, something happens which convinces your basic self to stop following that pattern.

That's exactly what we are doing here. Let's examine how such patterns are formed. Everyone's case is unique, of course, but in general, the three examples given above may have begun something like this:

(ALICE) Let's assume that this lady, who is now perhaps middle-aged, is indeed frequently ill, but her physician can find no medical reason for her recurring sicknesses.

If, as a three-year-old, or even earlier, Alice had repeatedly "learned" from her mother that "little girls in our family are always "frail and sickly," but, on the other hand, she also "learned" that "the women on our side of the family are all hard workers," that double message could be where her life-long problem began. Her basic self is caught in the middle of the conflict between those two perceptions—she *should* be a hard worker, but she *can't* because she is "sickly." The tension caused between "should" and "can't" is quite sufficient to keep Alice sad and ill.

(BILL) Bill might be any age from his late '20's to his early '50's. It could be that Bill's father had a money problem. He was always demonstrating that he was worried about the absolute necessity of being a "financial success" in life. Let's theorize that one day, long ago, when Bill had just joined the Cub Scouts, he goofed off and didn't do his assigned chores at home properly. His father gave him a very stern lecture, questioned his young son's ability to do anything right, and withheld his allowance. The father "drilled" it into Bill's impressionable mind that if he didn't always work hard and earn a lot of money, he would wind up on skid row "like those poor bums we saw down there the other day!" Growing up under that kind of fear-inducing indoctrination, Bill's basic self developed a very fixed attitude toward money and effort.

(CHARLOTTE) This lady is, let us say, in her early '30's. She is subconsciously attracted to a certain kind of man and always tries to be appealing to him. However, after a date or two—as soon as she indicates that she is serious—he leaves her. It could be that her father had always been cool and distant, ignoring his young daughter's natural need for affection. In her pre-adolescent years, her maladjusted father's problems—whatever they may have been—became so overwhelming to him that he deserted his wife and child. He left home. Little Charlotte's mother frequently reinforced the experience by labeling all men as "unreliable" and "deserters." The child inwardly fumed at the injustice of that concept which she accepted as a fact.

That may be how little Charlotte "learned" that the men in her life always leave her, and why adult Charlotte's basic self somehow seems to find men who will fulfill that expectation.

Our hypothetical subjects, Alice, Bill and Charlotte, are all suffering as a present reality from behavior patterns which they learned subconsciously many years ago when they were children.

If you have an obstructing complex, it is unique, of course. In all probability, however, its pattern(s) contains the same types of components as those described above.

With regard to *consciously learned patterns* (desirable habits), please note that they are essential to a person's survival, well-being and safety. Children necessarily learn how to feed themselves, go to the bathroom, cross the street safely, read, write, play games, ride a bike, get along with others, etc., etc., etc. (In other societies they may have to learn a different set of survival skills).

If you are now ready to disconnect from—release the importance of—some unconsciously learned behavior which is giving you trouble, continue with the next step.

Isolating The Complex's Components

Take the pattern apart. Untangle its components as follows:

(PROVOKING THOUGHT) Put it into a short statement as in the above examples.

(DRIVING EMOTION) Isolate the emotion(s) which accompanies the thought. Are you feeling grief? Fear? Anger? Guilt? What? (See outline of Vector Counseling Method).

(BEHAVIOR/STRESS) Now identify the specific behavior/stress component. As a result of your holding onto a fixated, provoking thought—with its attendant emotions—your body, back then, made an effort to do something or not to do something. Now, in present time, relax and let your mind wander back. What do you feel that something might have been? Was it to lash out, to flee, hide, disappear, succumb, freeze, hold still, wait, wrench free, expand, contract, let go of something, hold onto something, etc., etc., etc.

(PERMANENCE) Remember that it is the "nature" of your basic self to hold these patterned elements together, always, unless somehow it is persuaded to stop doing that.

Now that you have isolated the components of the complex, you have disentangled them. Are you ready to dispose of them—get rid of them permanently? If so, proceed.

Disposing of the Complex's Components

Visualize a fire pit in front of you. If you prefer, picture a waste basket, an electronic shredder, or a psychic vacuum cleaner—whatever imagery of a disposal mechanism may appeal to you.

Where in your body do you hold *that* thought, feel *those* emotions, experience *that* behavior/bodily stress, and cling to the accompanying *permanence*— the *"always"* or *"never?"* Are they in your head? Your shoulders? Your heart? Your stomach? All over? Now, in your imagination, go back to where you first experienced those components together. While you are "back there," to emphasize to your basic self that you are getting rid of those components, make very definite gestures with your hands to the part(s) of your body where each of those components of the complex seems to be residing. Imagine that you are pulling each one out, separately. With a dramatic gesture, throw each of them into your visualized fire pit or other disposal unit.

You thus let your basic self know that any attachment to that unwanted complex no longer exists, and is therefore not to be acted upon.

Now, come back "up" to current time and look at the experience which prompted this session. If it seems OK, you have completed this Vector session.

If not, go back to an earlier time in your life and have another look.

When it does feel OK, your basic self is now free to act or react appropriately—in cooperation with your conscious self—in your own best interest, in each life situation as it occurs.

Questions? Answers:

(1) When you are looking backward for the earliest time an incident occurred, if you can't recall things just as they actually happened, it is equally effective for you to make up a plausible incident, because you are only working with your own impressions of what happened. That earliest time could be as far back as the occasion of your birth (GIRL: *"They had their hearts set on my being a boy!"*).

It could be that while you were still in your mother's womb you received a definite message that you were not wanted (MOTHER to FATHER: *"It's all your fault, you drunken bum! You got me pregnant! I don't want this damned baby!"*).

Your earliest time could even be your recollection of some horrendous event in a previous incarnation where you had terribly wronged someone, or vice versa (PERSON: *"I'm deathly afraid of sharp instruments!"* or, *"I hate (some ethnic religious group) with a passion!".*

(2) If your basic self later sends "up" to your conscious self any additional parts of the complex which you have discarded, deal with them in the same way.

(3) If a totally different complex later reveals itself, handle it in the same way.

(4) If you feel any reluctance about letting go of any of the parts of your complex, examine what (perhaps foolish) value holding on to the complex might have for you. Ask yourself what does it prevent happening, or facilitate happening, etc? After you have answered that question, and if you still want to get rid of the complex, use the same procedure to get rid of the reason(s) why you feel you wanted to hold on to the complex.

(5) Some may say "Why dig into the past? Let's just deal with the present. Answer: We *are* dealing with the present. To the basic self the past and present are one. They are both "now."

(6) If this Vector method sounds slightly familiar to you, it admittedly includes simplified, useful elements from earlier concepts. However, it selectively integrates those with original discoveries, which during a 25-year development period, have proved to be highly effective.

   If Vector seems too quick and easy, you might want

to use the Vector procedure on why you feel that a method of disposing of your unwanted complexes should necessarily be long and difficult.

(7) If you feel that your complex is really due to the influence of some other person(s) in your life, please understand that after you have made the desired changes in your self, you will be sending out a different set of subliminal signals or "vibes." Thus, your interactions with other people will be altered accordingly.

(8) Note that Vector is unique in that it does not diagnose, make judgments, or give advice. It does not tell you what you "should" or "should not" do, say or think. It is taught to you only as a simple, empirical (in the non-pejorative sense), technique for effectively getting rid of your unwanted behavior patterns and attitudes; for dismantling any obstructions on your path. The idea is to free yourself to the point where you have a justified confidence in your own good judgment and decision-making ability.

(9) It would be counter productive to lay in any new, permanent beliefs or concepts to replace the ones you have discarded. Keep your prayer-affirmations quite distinct from any permanent "frozen" concepts which might, at a later date, interfere with your further spiritual growth.

After you have completed your discarding, and feel that you have cleared your path of any complexes, don't reflect and look back on what you have just done. Leave those former complexes in the waste basket or fire pit where you have put them.

Outline of Vector Counseling Method

1. Have you determined that you have a complex that you want to get rid of?

2. Look for the four components which form a complex:

   a. Provoking thought or perception
   b. Driving emotion
   c. Behavior / bodily stress
   d. Permanence: the "always" or "never" feeling

3. Find the complex's beginning. Look for the earliest time (specific or plausible) when you experienced those components together.

4. Isolate the complex's components.

   a. Thoughts, such as:

      1) Whenever I . . . Then I . . .
      2) I always . . .
      3) They always . . .
      4) The world is . . .
      5) People are never . . . etc., etc., etc.

   b. Emotions

SERENITY · JOY · EXHILERATION · ENTHUSIASM · INTEREST · BOREDOM · IRRITATION · PAIN · ANTAGONISM · RAGE (overt anger) · HATE (covert anger) · RESENTMENT · FEAR · SHAME · GUILT · GRIEF · APATHY

NEUTRAL

A desirable state. Just like the driver of an automobile in neutral gear, you can quickly shift—temporarily—to any position on the emotional scale which is appropriate to your current circumstance—without your being stuck there.

c. Behavior / stress. Attempts of your body to do something or to avoid doing something "back then." Examples:

    1) To strike out
    2) To flee, hide, disappear
    3) To succumb
    4) To freeze, hold still, wait
    5) To wrench free
    6) To expand or contract
    1) To get rid of something . . . etc., etc., etc.

d. Permanence: The complex's "always" or "never" feeling.

5. Dispose of the complex's components through imagery. See yourself "back then" as you use gestures to throw each component into an imaginary disposal unit—a fire, wastebasket, shredder or whatever.

6. Do you have any questions with the above procedure? Review "Questions? Answers:"

    This marks the end of this particular piece of Vector cleansing work. Thank your basic self for cooperating, and get on with your Huna prayer.

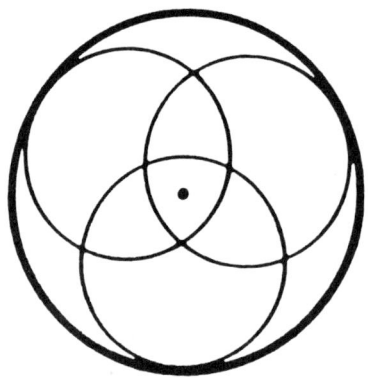

Vector Symbol

Chapter 14

Conducting the Ha Rite

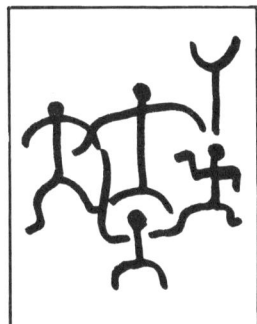

Choosing Your Setting

As a dramatic finale to the cleansing (kala) process, you might want to really take a bath. That symbology could be quite impressive to your basic self. Actually, no ritual is necessary. Our basic selves, however, are very responsive to drama, stage settings and ceremony. That is perhaps why many places of worship, such as temples, cathedrals and some churches are so beautifully elaborate, with carvings, stained glass windows, pictures, candles and incense.

If you want to designate a meditation place or altar area where you live, that's appropriate. If you choose to play some inspirational music, light a candle, ignite some incense, ring a bell or strike a gong and touch some water — a container of which you have placed on your altar and designated as holy — such procedures, while not really necessary, are symbolic and can contribute to your basic self's interest and eagerness to cooperate.

The candle flame can represent the spiritual light you are bringing into your life. The fragrant smoke rising from the incense can represent your prayer picture ascending to your high self. Water is the symbol for mana. The bell or gong is to alert your basic self to participate in the process, which may be thought of as a prayer, or a form of meditation.

Generating Mana

Whether you are seated before your altar, or at your favorite, secluded place in the woods, or by a quiet river, or even taking a break at your work place, close your eyes and relax. Let your conscious self tell your basic self, in effect, that you are, temporarily, taking charge of your body's breathing process, because rhythmic, deep breathing is the way to generate a greater than normal charge of mana. There are a lot of "right" ways to do deep breathing.

One simple and effective method is to take four deep breaths, holding each one, successively, for ten seconds and then exhale completely. As you breathe, visualize your body as a beautiful fountain, filling with water (our bodies are mostly water, anyway!). With each breath, visualize your body of water growing much, much larger — expanding exponentially (numbers successively multiplied by themselves).

Remember that the symbol for mana is water. Call on your imagination to "see" your surcharge of mana growing fantastically; from fountain-size to Olympic swimming pool size, on up to Great Lakes size and even to your favorite ocean—an ocean of mana to use in your ha rite.

Offering Up Mana

Silently, or aloud, have your conscious self instruct your basic self to activate the aka cord to your high self, and then send up that great surcharge of mana as an offering or sacrifice (the only kind of offering your high self wants). Do this by visualizing the accumulated mana rising from the great reservoir of your body, up your spine, through the top of your head, following the aka cord, on "up" to your high self — represented by a beautiful and powerful white light above you.

Adding Pictures

As your high self is absorbing the mana you are offering, you superimpose on it your prayer request — a healed body, a better income, a different job, a new car, an improved relationship, greater under-standing of life, or whatever.

It is essential that you clearly visualize a definite, positive picture of the changed condition as being a reality, an accomplished fact in your life. *Feel* it emo-tionally and *will* it to happen. Even as skilled arti-sans translate a blueprint of a house into an actual building, so your high self, in some mysterious way, converts your upsurging mana into mana loa and uses that to build your prayed-for condition into a reality for you.

Present your prayer request clearly, exactly the same way, three times, during each of your prayer sessions. Say it aloud, if appropriate in your surroundings.

As part of your prayer, be certain to visualize your high self providing you with a multi-level mantle of protection against any harm, by infusing your aura with a charge of powerful, white light (mana loa).

Giving Thanks

Conclude your prayer by giving thanks to your high self and to your basic self for the cooperation which they have given you. A Hawaiian conclusion to the prayer is, in English, approximately, "Thank you. Limitation is over. Let the prayer take its flight. Let the rain of blessings fall." In Hawaiian: *"Mahalo. Amama ua noa. Lele wale akua la"* (Mah-hah'-lo. Ah-ma-ma oo'-ah no'-ah. Lay-lay vah'-lay ah-koo'-ah lah'). As you conclude, visualize a fine mist of mana loa descending and forming a beautiful, multi-hued rainbow of protection and blessings all around you.

DIAGRAM OF A FAILED HA RITE

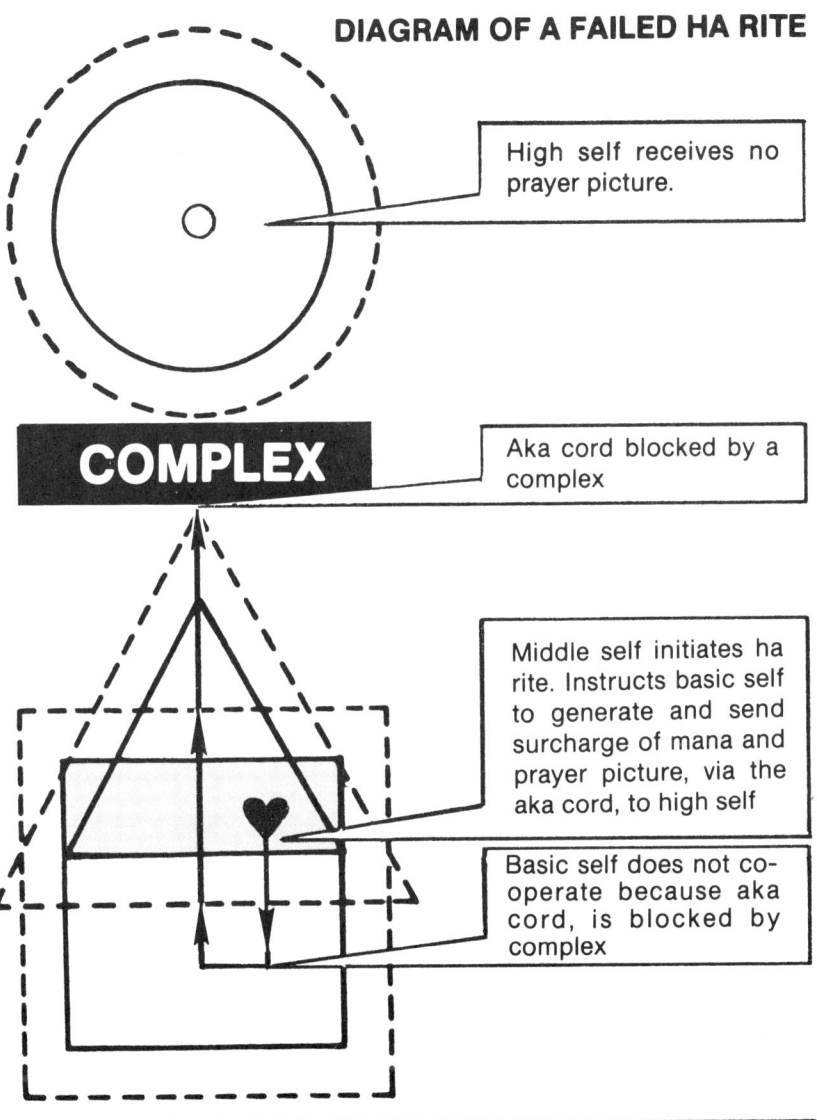

High self receives no prayer picture.

COMPLEX

Aka cord blocked by a complex

Middle self initiates ha rite. Instructs basic self to generate and send surcharge of mana and prayer picture, via the aka cord, to high self

Basic self does not co-operate because aka cord, is blocked by complex

RECAP OF THE PROBLEM OF THE COMPLEX: If a person's aka cord is blocked by a complex, the basic self will not cooperate with the middle self in sending a surcharge of mana, plus a prayer picture, to the high self.

DIAGRAM OF A SUCCESSFUL HA RITE

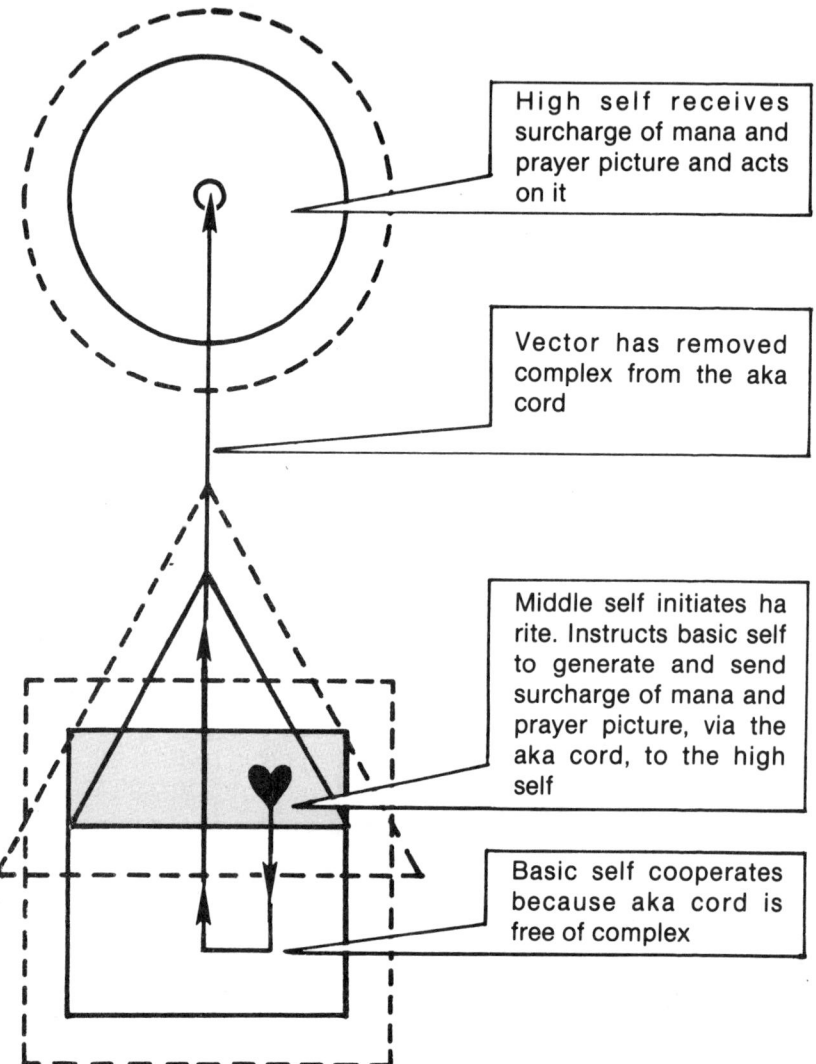

High self receives surcharge of mana and prayer picture and acts on it

Vector has removed complex from the aka cord

Middle self initiates ha rite. Instructs basic self to generate and send surcharge of mana and prayer picture, via the aka cord, to the high self

Basic self cooperates because aka cord is free of complex

RECAP OF THE SUCCESSFUL HA RITE: When a person's aka cord is complex-free, the basic self cooperates with the middle self in sending the surcharge of mana plus a prayer picture to the high self.

Flow Chart of the Ha Rite

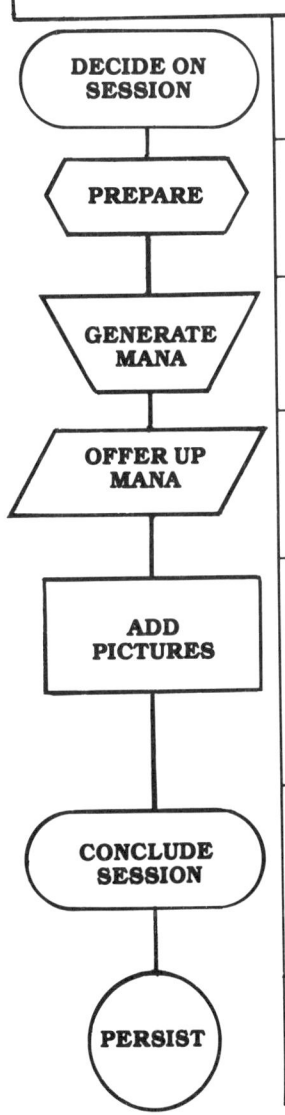

DECIDE ON SESSION	Whether it's your first time, an emergency or your regular procedure, you decide to make use of the ha rite.
PREPARE	Compose your prayer request carefully. Use Vector to dissolve any obstructing complexes. Choose your prayer time and place. Set an appropriate mood.
GENERATE MANA	Conscious self gets basic self's attention, then cooperation in using deep breathing procedure to generate a great surcharge of mana.
OFFER UP MANA	Conscious self relaxes and instructs basic self to begin sending that great surcharge of mana up the connecting *aka* cord as an offering to the high self.
ADD PICTURES	As the mana continues to rise, conscious self gets basic self to visualize positive, already-accomplished pictures of the prayed-for condition, and to superimpose those pictures on the ascending mana. State it, *feel* it, *will* it to become a reality. Repeat prayer, verbatim, three times.
CONCLUDE SESSION	In concluding, visualize your high self enveloping you in a protective aura of white light. Thank your high self and your basic self for its cooperation. Tell your basic self that this ha rite session is now ended.
PERSIST	Conduct repeat sessions of the ha rite as necessary, as though you are watering a seed which you have planted.

Chapter 15

Persisting/Insisting

Results? How Soon?

The time which it may take for your prayer request to become a reality can vary, depending on how effective your cleansing (kala) was and how well-conceived and well-pictured your prayer request was. Persist. Repeat your prayer three times a day, as you might take a valued prescription, or water a very special seed which you have planted in fertile, prepared soil. If your problem is acute, pray hourly. What you are doing is "watering" or nourishing with mana the prayer-seed which you planted.

Also, you must do the logical things that your prayer calls for. If you are seeking a healing, take all appropriate health measures. If you want a salary increase, do the necessary things to deserve it. If you are looking for a new relationship, be willing to participate in appropriate ways to meet people.

Sometimes your unwanted condition may seem to worsen a bit, temporarily, after you have started your prayer series. MFL explains that such an occurrence may be the result of your high self having to break up your old realities before building for you the new condition(s) which you have requested.

If your pictured prayer doesn't actualize as rapidly as you think it should, persist. Some results may take longer than others. Or, it may be that your high self knows that you are already committed to some longer-range master plan which will eventually work out for you more appropriately and more advantageously than you could have (subconsciously) anticipated.

Any "Eating Companions" Around

MFL attributed the ancient problem of possession to "eating companions"—mana stealing, disembodied entities—who are occasionally able to attach themselves to the shadow body of a "living" person's basic self, thus to participate vicariously in the hosts physical life. In the rare instance where the *kala* fails to exorcise such a parasite, the host may want to seek competent help.

Adjust your Karma?

As for karma, rejoice. On this pathway, *you* can decide when you have suffered enough for your past sins of hurting others. Any time you are ready, you will find your high self waiting to help you forgive and be forgiven; or, if you prefer, to accept and be accepted. As you become able to shed your anger, fear and guilt, together with whatever inappropriate, fixed concepts and stresses which may have been enslaving you, so will your karmic burden be correspondingly lightened, and your debt cancelled.

Chapter 16

Success Stories

The following paragraphs were submitted by friends/clients/ associates who had learned that I was writing this book. They wanted you to know of their success in using these techniques.

〰〰〰〰〰〰〰〰〰〰〰

My European childhood was one of great neglect and abuse. I grew up undereducated and harboring deep feelings of rage, fear, guilt and inadequacy. When I moved to Los Angeles a friend told me about Vector. That wonderful system enabled me to put my unhappy past behind me, to complete my college education (with good grades) and to attain my goal of becoming a registered nurse. In fact, I am now a special instructor of newly assigned nurses in a major Los Angeles hospital.

I continue to use both Vector and Huna in my daily life. As a woman of middle years, I am not exactly an athlete, but I love exercise and hiking. Each year I participate in our city's 26 mile marathon. Last year I finished near the end and was thoroughly exhausted. This year, I tried an experiment: as I passed each mile marker I made a point of generating an additional surcharge of mana. The result was remarkable! Not only did I feel less fatigue and muscle soreness, but I finished the course 45 minutes ahead of last year.

U.M., Los Angeles, CA

Huna unstuck three areas of my life. I didn't feel as well as I wanted to. My job was unpleasant. Someone hated me so much that I could feel it.

Now I say, "I am healthy, energetic and happy," and it's true!

I say, "On the job that's right for me, I sell well, feel self-confident and gain financially." I did find a much better job, do sell, my confidence soars. The money has bettered but not enough; I suspect I have something in the way and I need to work at that.

On the last problem, protection wraps around me daily. I feel completely free from outside negativity. As a bonus I experience feeling safer in my car, in any environment.

To sum it up, my life has improved astonishingly.

BJ, Long Beach, CA

I had a hard and bitter childhood in a country where life has been a struggle. When I came to the United States seeking a better way of life, I fortunately discovered Huna, and my life really has been getting better. My work is a very stressful job. I find Huna is a very effective method for dealing with this kind of stress and solving day-to-day problems.

M.I., Los Angeles, CA

One day, I made a fool of myself. I heard myself doing it but couldn't stop. A guest had arrived at our home forgetting that he had promised to bring us a certain article available in his town but not in ours. And I was whining—actually whining, telling him how I had counted on him to remember, so I hadn't phoned to remind him, and now I was going to have to drive over to his home town and blah, blah. I must have sounded—if not asinine—at least childish, and that night after the guest had left I remembered my behavior with chagrin.

At the next Vector group session, I recounted this irrational behavior. The leader, of course, asked me what my emotion was. I said, "Embarrassment."

"Wait a minute," he said, "not the emotion that resulted from the incident, but the emotion that provoked it."

"Disappointment".

"Of course," he said. "Now, the effort. What exactly were you trying to accomplish by this behavior?"

"I wanted him to feel bad."

"See what advantage—probably a silly advant-age—that would give you."

"Then he'd ---. I don't know."

"What was it you started to say?"

"It doesn't make sense; I was starting to say, 'Then he'd fix it'."

"Oh! Good one! Let's go with that."

It turned out that my belief was that "He would fix it," if I made him feel bad enough. My emotion was disappointment (at least, so I thought), and my effort was to make him feel bad. It took a little probing, but we got back to a childhood incident when I must have been three or younger. I was playing with one of my favorite toys, a truck. I was gleefully rolling it down my driveway and across the pavement into the grass between pavement and street. The man next door stepped from behind a hedge, and kicked the truck, tearing a wheel off its axle. His first response was to ask me what I expected if I left my truck on the sidewalk. But I was crying and saying things like "Look what you did," and "Now I can't play with my truck any more." Finally, the man took the truck and said he'd fix it. And he did. So it turned out that *my* version of "disappointment" was actually a kind of suppressed grief.

That was several years ago. Things often turn out to be less than I expected, but to this day I haven't felt disappointment. Not once!

BK, Harbor City, CA

As a semi-retired Los Angeles school teacher, I sometimes reflect on how Vector liberated me, several years ago, from a number of damaging beliefs foisted on me by my parents when I was a child. For example, I have always loved the idea of playing the piano, but for a long time I was puzzled by the fact that I would sit at the keyboard wanting to practice and wondering why I couldn't seem to get started.

After a friend introduced me to Vector, I was amazed to discover that, unconsciously, I still believed the threat of my parents that they would chop off my hands if I touched *their* piano again! After disposing of that gruesome concept, I began to enjoy my piano playing.

Subsequently, Vector helped me to remove a whole (unconscious) "storeroom" of untrue and unwanted beliefs caused by my parents who had constantly reminded me during my childhood that I was "good for nothing." Viva Vector!

S.H., California City, CA

After 12 years, the tragedy of losing my 16 year old daughter in a traffic accident still haunted me. The techniques in this book helped me almost immediately to accept this grief and get on with my life.

D.L., Granada Hills, CA

I was raised an Irish Catholic in New Zealand. Even as a child, however, I seemed to have an intuitive grasp of the power of the "magic" system which I later learned was Huna. Those principles worked in a most wondrous way to resolve seemingly insoluble problems at key points in my life and in the life of our family.

We were a young couple, living in Auckland, with our two small children, when my husband decided he must study chiropractic at a world famous college in California! Everyone tried to dissuade us. We were assured it would be many years before we could obtain the necessary emigration documents. Where would the money come from? Where would we live in a strange new country, etc., etc.

To shorten a long story, we used the Huna technique consistently and the obstacles fell away, one by one. We were moved from the bottom of the waiting list of emigres to the top. After we arrived in San Francisco, our money problem miraculously resolved itself. Soon after moving to Los Angeles, we were "led" to a charming home, *which we could afford to buy,* in a pleasant suburb. My husband completed his chiropractic training and established his practice in Los Angeles.

That was years ago. Now our children are grown, life goes on and we remain active in a local Huna group.
                                        JW, Pasadena, CA

As a long-time practitioner of the Huna philosophy, I compare my Huna prayers to a garden. Years ago, when I left the planting and nurturing of ideas and asperations (in my subconscious) to chance, I found my figurative garden overrun with weeds. That is, my subconscious dutifully sent those random pictures up to my high self. The result was that the outworking of events in my life was equally random and chancy.

Huna taught me to clearly define the thought-form "seeds" which I planted in the garden of my subconscious, and to "water" those "seeds" every day with mana. The result is a beautiful and very productive garden. That is, those properly nurtured thought-forms really grow into the desirable realities which I visualize. It works like magic.

Dr. M.C., Garden Grove, CA

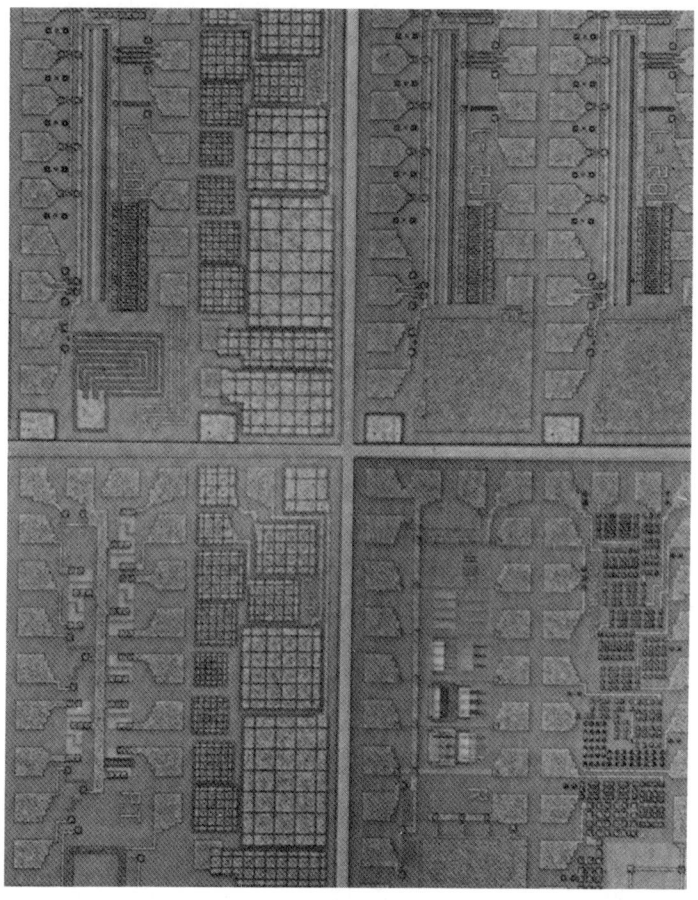

As you get the "bugs" out of its "integrated circuitry" you'll find your basic self becoming more "user friendly".

Chapter 17

Aloha Nui Loa

The purpose of this work has been to tell you, simply and briefly, about Huna—where it came from, what it is, and how to use mana; also, to introduce you to the unique Vector method of dismantling complexes.

When you have removed any undesirable obstructions from your path, you will find that you can make rapid progress toward the effective integration of your three "selves." That achievement will enable you to use the magic of Huna to direct your life into richly rewarding channels.

If you continue along this path after your immediate needs are met, you will find that you create a harmonious environment for yourself; one in which you can evolve meaningfully in an appropriate direction of your own choosing, and at your own pace.

If you want to inquire about additional information concerning Huna or Vector, or want help in applying these techniques, please see the Appendix.

The priceless, ancient secret is now yours. Use it wisely and prosper as you progress along "The Way."

Aloha Nui Loa means a loving farewell for now.

APPENDIX

Huna: Barnhart Press Information

To receive an updated list of Barnhart Press publications, send a business-sized envelope, self-addressed and stamped with first-class postage. You will receive a description of current offerings, including audio cassette demonstrations: a voice-assisted "walk-through" of the Vector counseling method and a complete presentation—explanation and enactment—of the formal Huna ha-rite.

Address your envelope to: Barnhart Press
Post Office Box 27940
Los Angeles, CA 90027

Huna Research Inc. Information

The books written by Max Freedom Long are:

Recovering the Ancient Magic

Introduction to Huna

The Secret Science Behind Miracles

The Secret Science at Work

Growing into Light

Self-Suggestion

Psychometric Analysis

The Huna Code in Religions

Mana, or Vital Force

Tarot Card Symbology

Short Talks on Huna

Huna Stories for Children

What Jesus Taught in Secret

To receive a complete list of all Huna-related publications, together with prices and an order form, send a business-sized envelope, self-addressed and stamped with first-class postage to: *Huna Research Inc., 1760 Anna Street, Cape Girardeau, MO 63701.*

If you want to inquire about a Huna Fellowship meeting near you, or a Huna counselor in your area, phone (314) 334-3478, between 9 a.m. and 5 p.m. weekdays, Central Time.

Vector Information

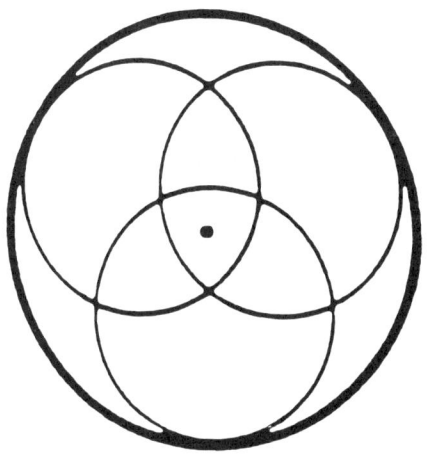

To receive a list of Vector publications, with prices, send a business-sized envelope, self-addressed and stamped with first class postage to: *The Vector Church, 1065 Lomita Blvd., #388, Harbor City, CA 90710.*

If you want to inquire about Vector counseling, in person or via telephone, call (213) 539-3922. If you call at a time when you may be answered by an electronic machine instead of by a real, live person, please leave your name, telephone number, city, state and the best times (your local time) for a Vector counselor to return your call, person-to-person, collect.

Glossary

Many Hawaiian words have more than one meaning, depending on the context in which they're used. The following definitions pertain only to the words' meanings as they apply in MFL Huna.

AKA   shadow; figure or outline

AKUA   a god; spelled with a capital A: Akua, the Christian God

ALII   chief (or chiefs)

ALO   flat land

ANA ANA   death prayer

AUMAKUA   one's high self, superconscious, guardian angel

COMPLEX   a rigid and unwanted concept, held on to firmly by the basic self. This blocks desired communications from the conscious self, via the basic self, to the high self

E HOOMAKA   begin

EATING COMPANIONS   disembodied entities who may, in some cases, be able to attach themselves to the aka body of a "living" person's basic self. Their purpose is to participate vicariously in some (low-level, probably addictive) aspect of that person's physical life

HA   breath

HA RITE   a huna prayer

HOOPONOPONO   a traditional, Hawaiian form of family/group therapy for resolving problems and making things right

HUNA   secret

KAHUNA   a general name which was applied to someone who had a profession or trade. In antiquity, unless otherwise specified, it was generally understood to refer to a priest (usually hereditary) who officiated at sacrifices. In spite of the term's present popularity, some authorities feel that the word is properly a historical term only and that the last real kahuna was Hewahewa who lived in the first half of the nineteenth century

KALA   a belief, Hindu/Buddhist and otherwise widely-held, of cause and effect; the concept that a person's actions inevitably produce corresponding appropriate consequences for that person (possibly in this life, or certainly) in a reincarnation

KANALOA a god; symbol of the ocean and fishing

KANE a god; symbol of life, nature, fresh water and sunlight

KIRLIAN PHOTOGRAPHY a process discovered by a Soviet couple, S.D. & V.K. Kirlian, whereby electrical charges emanating from living objects is recorded on photographic film as an aura-like glow

KU a god, symbol of war, chiefs, forests and canoe making

LA light

LONO a god; symbol of agriculture, clouds and weather

MAGIC (as used in "Mana Magic") a seemingly inexplicable power which can change things

MANA a generalized life force which may be concentrated in certain objects and in people, endowing those who possess it with extraordinary power

MANA MANA the conscious self's life force which makes rational thinking possible

MANA LOA the exponentially enhanced power used by the high self

MAOLI the original inhabitants of Hawaii; those who were there before the arrival of the Alii in the mid twelfth century

MU (1) a name which the original Hawaiians applied to themselves; (2) a lost continent which legend says sank into the SW Pacific Ocean in ancient times; also called Lemuria

POE AUMAKUA great company of high selves. Any group of high selves who might be networking on some project

REINCARNATION the belief that a person's soul (the three "selves" in Huna) lives on after physical death occurs and sooner or later is born on earth again (reincarnates) in a new body

UHANE the conscious or middle self

UNIHIPILI the subconscious, "low" or basic self

VECTOR in biology, a carrier; in mathematics, a quantity possessing both magnitude and direction. "Vector" was chosen by George Burtt as the name of the counseling system which he developed and incorporated in California in 1967 as the Vector (nonsectarian) Church

INDEX

3-5, 11-12

Atlantis, 15

51, 57, 59, 61, 62

Burtt, George, 41

Christian Science, 38

42-45, 47-54

conscious self, 27-29, 30-31, 59,
61-62

Dianetics, 38

Egypt, 15

God, 26, 31

Huna, 5-7, 23, 25, 39, 42, 75

Huna Research, Inc., 26

Kirlian photography, 28

16, 17, 19, 21, 23

Lemuria, 15

Long, Max Freedom, 4-6, 13, 23,
25-26

60

Maoli, 16, 19

Mu, 15

38

Vector, 7, 41-42, 50-54, 75

Tahitian Mask